easy Disney favorites

GW01158555

PLAY WITH THE PROS

Perform with recorded accompaniments by top professional musicians! The **Solo Trax**® book and CD will provice hours of entertaining and useful practice. Each song has a brief intro to establish the tempo and style. Be sure to "tune up" before you start. Listen and match the tuning notes so you'll blend nicely with the band. Remember, you're playing with the PROS!

ISBN 978-0-7935-9715-4

Walt Disney Music Company
Wonderland Music Company, Inc.

DISTRIBUTED BY

HAL•LEONARD®
CORPORATION

7777 W. BLUEMOUND RD. P.O. BOX 13819 MILWAUKEE, WI 53213

Visit Hal Leonard Online at
www.halleonard.com

NOTES YOU NEED TO KNOW

TIME VALUES YOU NEED TO KNOW

TIME
SIGNATURE

MICKEY MOUSE MARCH

Violin

Words and Music by
JIMMIE DODD

SUPERCALIFRAGILISTICEXPIALIDOCIOUS

(From Walt Disney's "MARY POPPINS")

Violin

Words and Music by
RICHARD M. SHERMAN and ROBERT B. SHERMAN

CHIM CHIM CHER-EE
(From Walt Disney's "MARY POPPINS")

Violin

Words and Music by
RICHARD M. SHERMAN and ROBERT B. SHERMAN

A DREAM IS A WISH YOUR HEART MAKES

(From Walt Disney's "CINDERELLA")

Violin

Words and Music by MACK DAVID,
AL HOFFMAN and JERRY LIVINGSTON

A SPOONFUL OF SUGAR

Violin

Words and Music by
RICHARD M. SHERMAN and ROBERT B. SHERMAN

WINNIE THE POOH

Violin

Words and Music by
RICHARD M. SHERMAN and ROBERT B. SHERMAN

ZIP-A-DEE-DOO-DAH

Violin

Words by RAY GILBERT
Music by ALLIE WRUBEL

THE WORK SONG

Violin

Words and Music by MACK DAVID,
AL HOFFMAN and JERRY LIVINGSTON

CANDLE ON THE WATER
(From Walt Disney Productions "PETE'S DRAGON")

Violin

Words and Music by
AL KASHA and JOEL HIRSCHHORN

BIBBIDI-BOBBIDI-BOO
(From Walt Disney's "CINDERELLA")

Words by JERRY LIVINGSTON
Music by MACK DAVID and AL HOFFMAN

Violin

Brightly (In Two)

LET'S GO FLY A KITE

Violin

Words and Music by
RICHARD M. SHERMAN and ROBERT B. SHERMAN

TOYLAND MARCH

Words by MEL LEVEN
Music by GEORGE BRUNS
(Adapt. From V. Herbert Melody)

Violin

March Tempo

IT'S A SMALL WORLD
(Theme From the Disneyland and Walt Disney World Attraction, "IT'S A SMALL WORLD")

Violin

Words and Music by
RICHARD M. SHERMAN and ROBERT B. SHERMAN